Mass
Appeal

Mass Appeal
Jimmy Akin
Second, revised edition © 2003, 2011 by Catholic Answers

Mass Appeal is the ideal tool to explain "the source and summit of the Christian Life" (LG 11) to a wide range of individuals and groups, including parish study groups, RCIA classes, upper-grade CCD classes, and non-Catholics curious about our rich liturgy. The booklet also is a valuable addition to literature racks at your church. Make a gift to your parish of a copy for each family.

Published by
Catholic Answers, Inc.
P.O. Box 199000, San Diego, California 92159-9000
1-888-291-8000 (U.S. orders) 619-387-7200 (international orders)
www.catholic.com

Cover design by Devin Schadt
Interior design Russell Design
Printed in the United States of America
ISBN 978-1-888992-32-8

Nihil Obstat
I have concluded that the materials presented in this work
are free of doctrinal or moral errors.
Bernadeane Carr, STL
20 September 2011

Imprimatur
In accord with 1983 CIC 827 § 3, permission to publish this work is hereby granted.
†Robert H. Brom
Bishop of San Diego
20 September 2011

Mass
Appeal

The ABCs of Worship

JIMMY AKIN

Catholic
Answers
Press

CONTENTS

Dedication

For "Fatima,"
who inspired me to write
this guide to the Mass.

1. INTRODUCTION

The Mass is the most important form of Christian worship. All worship is meant to draw us closer to God, and the Mass is special, not only because we approach God in it, but because he also approaches us. In the Mass, Jesus Christ comes to meet us in a unique way.

This booklet is for people who want to get more out of Mass, both those who have been going all their lives and those who are just starting to go. We will discuss in a general way what the Mass is, why it takes place, and how to appreciate it more. We will also look specifically at the things and people you see there, as well as the parts of the Mass—why they are there, and what they mean.

If you have been going to Mass all your life, you already have a sense of what it is like to participate in the liturgy. You already know *what* happens. This booklet will help you learn more about *why* it happens. You will also be intrigued to learn the names and purposes for things you have seen all your life. You will see how the pieces fit together, how the Mass makes a single, coherent whole.

If you are encountering the Mass for the first time, you may find it a little hard to absorb all that is going on, because the liturgy is a rich experience that includes forms of worship that go back to Jesus and the apostles. This booklet will help you learn, recognize, and understand the parts of the Mass and what they mean.

Do not think that you have to memorize everything in this booklet. It is meant as a guide to help you identify and understand things, as well as give you background. You can refer to this booklet later to refresh your memory, but there is no need to memorize all the names and facts in it.

A special word to those who are learning about the Mass for the first time: Because the Mass is so rich, the first few times you attend, you may just want to *observe*—until you understand more and feel more comfortable participating. That is fine. Everybody has to learn about the Mass sometime, and nobody will think ill of you if you do not do what everyone else is doing while you are still learning.

You may want to stand when others stand, kneel when they kneel, and shake hands when they shake hands. Or you may simply want to sit and watch. Just do as much as you are comfortable doing as you learn to appreciate the beauty and subtlety of the Mass and how it can bring you closer to God.

You may want to follow along with a printed text—such as this booklet—or a *missal* or a *missalette*, which have the actual words of the Mass in them. (We will learn more about these two, below.)

If you are not used to the kind of worship done at Mass, do not let it bother you. Go at your own pace. God wants you to learn to appreciate the richness of the Mass in a way that draws you closer to him. If you are distracted—trying to keep track of too many things—terms, prayers, actions, meanings—then relax. As you attend, God will help you enjoy more parts of the Mass. You will find yourself growing ever closer to him and learning more about him.

He loves you.

That is why he gave us the Mass.

2. THE MASS AS WORSHIP

The Mass is a form of *worship*, which is how we proclaim God's greatness and our need for him. The worship that we give to God is also called *adoration*. The *Catechism of the Catholic Church* gives an excellent explanation:

> Adoration is the first act of the virtue of religion. To adore God is to acknowledge him as God, as the Creator and Savior, the Lord and Master of everything that exists, as infinite and merciful Love. "You shall worship the Lord your God, and him only shall you serve," says Jesus [Luke 4:8], citing Deuteronomy [6:13].
>
> To adore God is to acknowledge, in respect and absolute submission, the "nothingness of the creature" who would not exist but for God. To adore God is to praise and exalt him and to humble oneself, as Mary did in the Magnificat, confessing with gratitude that he has done great things and holy is his name [cf. Luke 1:46-49]. The worship of the one God sets man free from turning in on himself, from the slavery of sin and the idolatry of the world (CCC 2096-2097).

Worship can be expressed in many different ways. Anything that expresses the truth about God is a form of worship, and Christians have worked out many methods of worship. Some are loud and energetic, others are quiet and solemn. This is as it should be, because God has designed us so that experience different moods. Sometimes we want to praise God energetically; sometimes we want to praise God quietly and solemnly. Catholic worship embraces both of these styles, as well as mixtures of the two.

A characteristic of some forms of worship is spontaneity. It is unscripted. Given what the worshiper feels, he decides at the moment how best to praise God. A characteristic of other forms of worship is that they are regular and predictable. This predictability in worship is often called *ritual*.

Worship can be either private or public, for God has designed us to function both as individuals and as part of a group. We are social creatures; it is not good for us always to be or to act alone (Genesis 2:18). The public aspect of worship requires more ritual, because when people worship as a group, they need to know what to expect, what comes next. The larger the group, the greater the need for ritual.

Whenever people get together in a group, there are leaders. At Mass, these are the priests. In the New Testament, they are referred to as *presbyters,* or *elders*. Indeed, the English word *priest* is taken from the Greek word for elder, *presbuteros*. The priests represents the people to God and Christ to the people.

When worship is conducted on behalf of the people, it can become *liturgy*. Liturgy is the official worship of the Church on behalf of the faithful. "In Christian tradition it means the participation of people of God in 'the work of God.' " (CCC 1069).

Whenever the seven sacraments are celebrated, a liturgy is being performed. Each involves the worship of God for the benefit of the people. The most important is the *Eucharist*, because in this sacrament Jesus Christ himself comes to meet with the faithful.

A word that you will hear a number of times during Mass is *sacrifice*. The idea of sacrifice is deep, but in the most basic sense a sacrifice occurs whenever something is offered to God. In the Eucharist, Jesus as the high priest of all Christians (Hebrews 4:14) presents himself to the Father on our behalf. He is always praying for us

(Hebrews 7:25, 1 John 2:1), asking the Father to be merciful to us on account of his death on the cross.

In many sacrifices we read about in the Bible, though not all, the gift presented to God dies. This happened to Jesus when he was sacrificed on the cross, but it does not happen to him in the Eucharist, for Christ "died for sins once for all" (1 Peter 3:18). Instead, Christ today represents and offers himself to the Father as a *living* sacrifice, which Paul says all Christians should do (Romans 12:1).

Scripture depicts the liturgy conducted on earth as an image of the life of *heaven*. Both are said to involve priests (Exodus 28:1, Romans 15:16, Hebrews 8:1), altars (Exodus 29:12–14, Malachi 1:12, 1 Corinthians 10:21, Revelation 8:3–5), incense (Exodus 30:1, Revelation 5:8), and set prayer responses (Psalm 136, 1 Corinthians 11:23–25, 14:16, Revelation 4:8–11). In the Bible, corporate worship, like heavenly worship, is ritual in nature. By participating in the liturgy, we are united to the continual worship of God in heaven (CCC 1326). This is done in a special way in the Eucharist, because Jesus is both in heaven and in our midst in the Eucharist. Our joining with the heavenly worship of God gives us a foretaste of heaven. Only there will we be able to worship God and experience him and his greatness fully, free of the distractions that hamper our worship here on earth.

3. WHAT YOU SEE IN CHURCH

Even before Mass starts, there are many things you see in church. Just as there are reasons for the different parts of the Mass, there are also reasons for these things.

Holy water is placed at the entrance of the church to remind us that through baptism we entered the Church.

In some parishes, the actual *baptismal font* itself is used for this purpose.

Otherwise, just inside the entrance are *holy water fonts*. These are small containers for water that has been blessed by a priest or a deacon. Holy water has been used since biblical days (Numbers 5:17), and today people customarily bless themselves with holy water as a reminder of their baptism.

Dipping their fingers in the holy water, they make the sign of the cross while saying part of the words used in baptism: "In the name of the Father and of the Son and of the Holy Spirit" (Matthew 28:19).

Those who are not yet baptized can do this as a way of looking forward to their baptism.

You will also notice *candles* in church. These not only provide light; they also serve as symbols. They may, for example, symbolize the teaching of Christ, "the light of the world" (John 8:12). They also symbolize prayer. When people who are praying about a special matter would like to stay in church but can not, they often light a candle as a symbol of their prayer.

Another symbol of prayer you sometimes see in church is *incense*. Because the smoke of incense floats upward, it has been used since biblical times to symbolize our prayers rising before God (Revelation 5:8, 8:3–4).

There are also *statues*, carvings, and pictures of saints and angels in the church. This custom goes back to the Bible, when God commanded the Israelites to fill their places of worship with images of angels (Exodus 25:18–20, 1 Chronicles 28:18–19, Ezekiel 41:17-20). This was because the holy places symbolize heaven, and to remind men of this, God had them place representations of the inhabitants of heaven in them. Since Jesus has opened the gates of heaven, human souls now go there. That is why we now have statues of human saints as well as angels.

The main body of the church, where the people sit, is called the *nave*. In most churches the nave is filled with long benches, or *pews* with kneelers. In the pews you will often find a number of books that may be used during Mass. One of these is a *missal*, a book containing the words of the readings and prayers used at Mass. If a missal is not available, there will often be a *missalette*, essentially a smaller version of a missal, covering only the current season in the Church's calendar. There may also be a *hymnal* containing songs and hymns.

The other main part of the church is called the *sanctuary*. It is the place where the priests, deacons, and other ministers perform their jobs at Mass.

One of the things you will see in the sanctuary is the place from which Scripture is read. This is called the *ambo*, or *lectern*.

The central furnishing in the sanctuary is the *altar*, where the priest celebrates the Eucharist. Ever since biblical times, the altar has been referred to as "the table of the Lord" (Malachi 1:7, 12; 1 Corinthians 10:21), which is why offerings such as the Eucharist are made there. To show their reverence for the table of the Lord, people *bow* their heads when they pass in front of an altar.

On the altar are *vessels* used during the Eucharist, such as the *ciborium*, a plate or dish-like vessel, and the *chalice*, a goblet or cup-like vessel. These are made of precious material because they will hold the Body and Blood of Christ. Also on the altar is a book called the

Roman Missal, which contains the prayers that the priest uses during Mass—the same prayers found in a missal or missalette found in the pews.

On or near the altar is a crucifix—a cross with an image of Christ crucified. The crucifix serves as a visible reminder that Christ loved us so much that he died in order that our sins might be forgiven (John 3:16, Galatians 2:20).

The *tabernacle* is a vessel in which the Eucharist is kept for the devotion of the faithful and so that it may be taken to the sick. The tabernacle is like the biblical Ark of the Covenant that held the manna God sent from heaven for the Israelites to eat (Exodus 16:4). Jesus in the Eucharist is the manna that God has sent from heaven for Christians to eat (John 6:32, 41). In this way the tabernacle that holds the Eucharist is like the Ark of the Covenant.

In many churches the tabernacle is placed on an altar in the sanctuary. In others it is placed in a separate chapel. To show their respect for Jesus, people *genuflect*—kneel briefly on the right knee—when they pass in front of the tabernacle unless they are moving in procession.

4. PEOPLE IN CHURCH

Most of the people at Mass are ordinary members of the faithful. They are called the *laity*, which simply means "the people." A few of the people at Mass are members of the *clergy*—that is, bishops, priests, and deacons.

Bishops are the successors of the original apostles. A bishop shepherds all of the local congregations, or *parishes*, in a given region. Because there are more parishes than there are bishops, they cannot be at every Mass, so it is a special occasion when a bishop comes to celebrate a Mass at a particular parish.

The highest clergyman at most Masses is a *priest*. These men shepherd individual parishes or congregations. Each parish is entrusted specifically to one priest, known as the *pastor* (Latin, "shepherd"). Often he is assisted in his parish ministry by other priests, who are *associate pastors*. Priests administer most of the sacraments of the Church. The one most central to their ministry is the Eucharist.

During Mass, you can recognize a priest because he wears a long piece of cloth—called a *stole*—over both his shoulders. If more than one priest is celebrating the Mass, each wears a stole. The main priest celebrating a Mass, however, wears another large piece of cloth, called a *chasuble,* which covers his shoulders, chest, and back. He wears it even if he is the only priest at Mass.

The *colors* of these articles of clothing—or *vestments*—vary according to what season or day it is in the Church's calendar. They may be green, for ordinary time; purple, for the seasons of Advent and Lent; white, for the seasons of special joy (Christmas and Easter) and special days of celebration; or red, on days such as Pentecost or for the memorial days of martyrs.

Bishops and priests are assisted in their ministry by *deacons*. These men also have received the sacrament of holy orders. They often perform baptisms serve as the Church's representative at marriages, and conduct funerals. Though they are not able to consecrate the Eucharist, deacons often assist priests at Mass. You can recognize a deacon at Mass because he wears a stole over one shoulder, not over both as a priest does.

In addition to the clergy who perform official functions at Mass, certain lay people do as well. For example, at many Masses a lay person proclaims the Scripture readings except for the gospel, which is reserved to a bishop, priest, or deacon. This person is called a *lector* (Latin, "reader").

Another layperson who may serve at Mass is an altar server who assists the priest, for example, by handing him the things he needs at different points in the Mass. Altar servers are usually drawn from the young people of the parish. Hence they are often known as altar boys or altar girls.

When it is time for Communion, the ordinary ministers of Communion are bishops, priests, and deacons. Some parishes are so large, however, that there are not enough of these individuals. The Blessed Sacrament is then distributed by *extraordinary ministers of Holy Communion.*

There is also a special group of individuals who may help with the singing and music at Mass. These include the *cantor* (Latin, "singer").

5. OVERVIEW OF THE MASS

The two largest and most important parts of the Mass are the *Liturgy of the Word* and the *Liturgy of the Eucharist.* The Liturgy of the Word is the part of the service in which God's word is read and preached. The Liturgy of the Eucharist is the part of the service in which the Eucharist is consecrated and Communion is distributed.

These two liturgies form the core of the Mass. They are its most important parts, though there also are brief *Introductory Rites* before the Liturgy of the Word and brief *Concluding Rites* after the Liturgy of the Eucharist. Thus the Mass has a four-part structure:

I.   Introductory Rites
II. The Liturgy of the Word
III. The Liturgy of the Eucharist
IV. Concluding Rites

If you can keep these four divisions in mind, you know the basic structure of the Mass. If you are just learning the Mass, focus on these four parts. Everything that happens at Mass fits into one of them. They are the keys to seeing how the individual parts fit together to form a whole.

Though the details of various parts of the Mass have changed over the centuries, its basic structure has always been the same. It goes back to the very dawn of Christian history. Around A.D. 155, Justin Martyr wrote about how Mass was celebrated in his day:

All [Christians] who dwell in the city or country gather in the same place.

The memoirs of the apostles and the writings of the prophets are read, as much as time permits.

When the reader has finished, he who presides over those gathered admonishes and challenges them to imitate these beautiful things.

Then we all rise together and offer prayers* for ourselves . . . and for all others, wherever they may be, so that we may be found righteous by our life and actions, and faithful to the commandments, so as to obtain eternal salvation.

When the prayers are concluded we exchange the kiss [of peace].

Then someone brings bread and a cup of water and wine mixed together to him who presides over the brethren.

He takes them and offers praise and glory to the Father of the universe, through the name of the Son and of the Holy Spirit and for a considerable time he gives thanks (in Greek: eucharistian) that we have been judged worthy of these gifts.

When he has concluded the prayers and thanksgivings, all present give voice to an acclamation by saying: "Amen."

When he who presides has given thanks and the people have responded, those whom we call deacons give to those present the "eucharisted" bread, wine and water and take them to those who are absent [CCC 1345, quoting Justin Martyr, First Apology 65–67; the text before the asterisk (*) is from chapter 67].

This same fundamental structure is preserved in the Mass of today: All gather; Scripture is read; preaching is done on the readings; prayers are offered; a sign of peace is exchanged among the faithful (in Justin Martyr's day this was a kiss, as in the New Testament: Romans 16:16, 1 Corinthians 16:20, 1 Peter 5:14); the elements to be consecrated are brought, the priest consecrates them in prayer; the faithful respond, "Amen"; and Communion is distributed.

It is impressive to see how the fundamental structure of Christian worship has remained the same through all the centuries.

Now we will look at the parts of the Mass in more detail.

6. THE PARTS OF THE MASS

I. INTRODUCTORY RITES

The purpose of the Introductory Rites is to prepare for the celebration of the Liturgy of the Word and the Liturgy of the Eucharist. These rites express the fact that the parish is coming together for worship, that we need to be purified for worship by remembering our sins and asking for God's mercy, and that we wish to give glory to God and ask him to bless our worship.

A. *Entrance* (Latin, *Introit*, "He enters"). Mass begins when the priest who will celebrate Mass enters the church and approaches the altar. Often others who will serve with him (such as deacon, lector, and altar servers) will accompany him. At this point, in Masses with music, the choir or the congregation will usually sing.

B. *Veneration of the Altar.* As the priest arrives at the altar, he venerates it, kissing it as a sign of reverence to God for the place where Jesus Christ will become present in the Eucharist. At some Masses, the priest incenses the altar as a symbol of reverence and prayer.

C. *Greeting.* The priest and the people make the sign of the cross as the priest calls upon God with the words "In the name of the Father and of the Son and of the Holy Spirit," to which the people respond, "Amen." This reminder of baptism serves to consecrate our actions to God. Afterwards the priest greets the people by wishing them God's grace or simply by saying, "The Lord be with you," to which the people respond, "And with your spirit."

D. *Penitential Act.* The priest then exhorts the people to prepare to worship God by recalling their sins, repenting of them, and asking for God's mercy. During a brief moment of silence, the people think about their sins, and then they pray together. Different prayers from the *missal or missalette* are used at this point. One of the most common begins with the words "I confess to almighty God, and to you, my brothers and sisters, that I have sinned through my own fault."

E. *Kyrie* (Greek, *Kyrie, Eleison,* "Lord, have mercy"). The acknowledgment of our sins concludes by asking God for his forgiveness. At this point the people pray to the Lord Jesus, "Lord, have mercy. Christ, have mercy. Lord, have mercy." Sometimes this is sung, and sometimes it is said in Greek: "*Kyrie, eleison. Christe, eleison. Kyrie, eleison.*" Before Latin became more common, Greek was the language most often used for celebrating Mass in the Church's earliest centuries.

F. *Blessing and Sprinkling* (Latin, *Asperges,* "You will sprinkle"). At some Masses a rite known as Blessing and Sprinkling is performed. It takes the place of the Penitential Act and the "Lord, Have Mercy."

The priest asks God to bless some water, making holy water. He then sprinkles the congregation with it. This action recalls our baptism, through which we were cleansed from sin (Acts 2:38, 22:16), and other biblical rituals, such as when the Psalmist prays, "Wash me thoroughly from my iniquity, and cleanse me from my sin!" (Psalms 51:2; see also Ezekiel 36:25–27).

G. *Gloria.* After having purified our hearts by recalling our sins and asking God's mercy, it is a moment for praise, and so in many Masses a prayer known as the *Gloria* (its first word in Latin) is said. It begins "Glory to God in the highest, and on earth peace to people of good will."

H. *Collect.* The priest then brings the Introductory

Rites to a close by saying to the people, "Let us pray." He then says the opening prayer, which is called the *collect*. There are different collects for different Masses and days of the year. Collects thank God, ask his blessing, and frequently introduce the themes that will be part of that day's Mass. Afterwards, all respond "Amen."

Following the Introductory Rites, the Liturgy of the Word begins.

II. THE LITURGY OF THE WORD

A. *Scripture Readings.* Since this part of the Mass is focused on hearing God's word, it naturally begins with a series of Scripture readings. There are always at least two readings, but on Sundays and certain holy days there are three, including the Gospel reading. The first is drawn from the Old Testament (except during the Easter season). Afterwards the lector says, "[This is] the word of the Lord," and all reply, "Thanks be to God."

After the reading, one of the Old Testament psalms (or another biblical prayer) is said or sung. It is done in a *responsorial* style—that is, the people singing it alternate, one group *responding* to what has just been sung by the other. Typically, the cantor sings a part of the psalm and the people give a response (like a refrain in a song). This alternating style in worship goes back to before the time of Christ, when it was used in the Jerusalem Temple (for example, with Psalm 136, whose refrain is "His mercy endures forever").

The second reading at a Sunday Mass is drawn from the New Testament. It can come from any of the New Testament books except the Gospels. Afterwards, the lector and the people make the same reply as at the end of the first reading.

Then comes the reading of the Gospel. Because the Gospels contain the actual story of the life of Christ, the reading of the Gospel is especially solemn this is reflected in a number of ways. Before the reading, during most of the year, an Alleluia (Hebrew, *Hallelujah!,* "Praise the Lord!") is said or sung. The reading itself is done only by a bishop, priest, or deacon; and during the reading, everyone stands as a sign of respect for Christ. Afterwards the reader says, "[This is] the Gospel of the Lord," and all respond, "Praise to you, Lord Jesus Christ."

B. *Homily.* Once the readings are completed, a *homily* may be given. A homily is preached to help the people understand the readings and how to apply them to their own lives. Homilies, always given on Sundays and certain other days, are recommended at ordinary weekday Masses as well. A bishop, priest, or deacon gives the homily.

C. *Profession of Faith* (*Creed*). The purpose of reading and preaching on Scripture is to help the faithful grow in the faith. After these two tasks are done, it is natural to express one's faith by a formal assent of faith. This is done on Sundays and certain other days by having a formal Profession of Faith, in which everyone recites a creed.

At many Masses, the particular Profession of Faith used is the *Nicene Creed.* It begins "I believe in one God, the Father almighty, maker of heaven and earth, of all things visible and invisible." This is an ancient creed and is based on even earlier creeds. The first part of it was written in a.d. 325 at a gathering of bishops known as the First Council of Nicaea. The last part of it was written in a.d. 381 at a similar gathering known as the First Council of Constantinople. It proclaims the core doctrines of the Christian faith, especially the Trinity (that God is one being in three Persons: the Father, the Son, and the Holy Spirit), and that Christ died for our sins and rose from the dead that we might have eternal life.

At other Masses, especially during Lent and Easter Time, the Profession of Faith used is the Apostles Creed. It begins: "I believe in God, the Father almighty, Creator of heaven and earth, and in Jesus Christ, his only Son, our Lord." This is also the creed used at baptism.

D. *Universal Prayer.* The faith is not only something to be believed; it is also something to be lived, such as by helping others—both fellow Christians and non-Christians. One way of doing this is to pray for them. That is why the Liturgy of the Word concludes with the Prayer of the Faithful, in which the whole assembly prays for various people and their needs. This form of prayer is called *intercessory prayer* (since the people are interceding with God on behalf of others), so this part of the Mass is also sometimes called the *Prayer of the Faithful* or *Bidding Prayers.*

How the Prayer of the Faithful is done varies from parish to parish and from Mass to Mass. The priest invites the prayer of the faithful and he or a deacon, cantor, or other person announces various prayer concerns, or *intentions*, to which the people pray a response such as "Lord, hear our prayer."

III. THE LITURGY OF THE EUCHARIST

After the Liturgy of the Word, in which we hear God's word and learn about him, comes the Liturgy of the Eucharist, in which we receive Communion and meet God bodily. Man has both a mind and a body, and this part of the Mass makes God real to us in a way that the mind alone could ignore or dismiss. The Eucharist goes beyond hearing and understanding the word and completes it in a way that the whole person—body as well as mind—is engaged and drawn to God.

A. *Preparation of the Gifts.* In the first part of the Liturgy of the Eucharist, the gifts of the faithful are prepared. This is also called the *Offertory* because here the gifts are brought to the altar. At this point the collection, if there is one, is taken up, as one of the people's gifts to God. Even more important, this is when the bread and wine given by God and worked by human hands are brought forward to be used by God in the Eucharist. Often this is done by members of the congregation.

B. *Prayer over the Offerings.* After the offerings have been received, the priest prays over them, asking God to bless them. In particular, he asks God to bless the bread and the wine that will be used in the Eucharist. After both of these prayers of blessing, the people respond, "Blessed be God forever."

During this time the priest also pours a little water into the wine in the chalice. This symbolizes the Incarnation of Christ. The water, representing humanity, is united to the wine, representing Christ's divinity. The priest also quietly says a prayer at this point. He asks that just as Christ became like us in having humanity, we might be made divine—in the sense that God lets us share certain of his attributes, such as righteousness and holiness (see 2 Peter 1:4). We cannot, of course, take on a divine nature in the way the Son took on a human nature.

Afterwards the priest washes his hands in water. This rite is known as the *Lavabo* (Latin, "I will wash"). Its meaning is brought out by the prayer he quietly says: "Wash me, O Lord, from my iniquity, and cleanse me from my sin." The priest is asking, in essence, for God to make him worthy to celebrate the Eucharist.

The priest also asks the people to pray that God will receive the sacrifice with favor, to which all reply, "May the Lord accept the sacrifice at your hands, for the praise and glory of his name, for our good, and the good of all his holy Church." The reason for this prayer is that, although Jesus Christ's gift of himself to the Father is *always* acceptable to God, our own limitations and weaknesses may prevent our actions from being pleasing to God. Thus, in spite of our weakness and sin, we ask God to look favorably on our worship.

C. *Eucharistic Prayer*. The priest then begins the eucharistic prayer. This is the most solemn part of the Mass. There are several eucharistic prayers that the Church uses. All of them follow the same basic structure. We will look at those used in the Latin (Roman) Rite of the Church.

1. *Thanksgiving (Preface)*. The eucharistic prayer begins with a thanksgiving offered to God. Indeed, it is thanksgiving that gives the Eucharist its name (Greek, *eucharistia,* "thanks"). This thanksgiving begins with a short dialogue between the priest and the people:

Priest: The Lord be with you.

People: And with your spirit.

Priest: Lift up your hearts [i.e., in prayer].

People: We lift them up to the Lord.

Priest: Let us give thanks to the Lord, our God.

People: It is right and just [i.e., to give him thanks].

After this dialogue, the priest gives thanks to God

for his saving acts. This follows the common pattern of thanking God for what he has already done for us before moving on to ask him to do new things for us.

2. *Acclamation (Sanctus)*. Following the thanksgiving, all present sing or say the acclamation known as the *Sanctus* (Latin, "Holy"):

Holy, holy, holy, Lord God of hosts, heaven and earth are full of your glory. Hosanna in the highest. Blessed is he who comes in the name of the Lord. Hosanna in the highest.

This joins the prayer of the congregation to the prayer of the angels in heaven, whom the Bible represents as singing of God's supreme holiness with the prayer "Holy, holy, holy" (Isaiah 6:3, Revelation 4:8).

Hosanna is a Hebrew term that originally meant "O, save [us]!" but came to be used as a shout of joy. The second part of this prayer recalls the words that the people cried out at Jesus' triumphal entry into Jerusalem (Matthew 21:9, Mark 11:9, John 12:13). Jesus also linked these words with his Second Coming (Matthew 23:39, Luke 13:35). By praying them now, we praise Jesus upon his eucharistic entry into the Mass and pray for his Second Coming.

3. *Epiclesis*. Afterwards, all kneel as a sign of reverence for Christ, and the priest calls upon God to send his Spirit upon the bread and wine so that they may become the body and blood of Jesus Christ. This part of the Mass is called the *epiclesis*, from a Greek word meaning "calling down upon." Often in parishes a *bell* is rung to signal that the most important part of the Mass is beginning.

4. *Institution Narrative and Consecration*. Next comes the part of the Mass in which the priest recalls the very

first Mass itself as part of the Last Supper on the night that Jesus was betrayed. The priest repeats what Jesus himself said on that night: "This is my body," and "This is the chalice of my blood." As the priest says these words, God performs a miracle that transforms the elements of bread and wine into the body and blood of Jesus Christ, together with his soul and his divinity. It is at this point that Jesus becomes really present in the Eucharist, the most unique way he comes to us in the present age.

Frequently in parishes a bell is rung after the Consecration. After Christ has become present in the hosts and in the chalice, the priest holds them up so that the people may see them and worship Jesus.

5. *Memorial Acclamation.* Because of this great mystery, the priest or deacon then says, "The mystery of faith." The people then repeat one of several prayers commemorating what Christ has done for us; for example, the prayer, "When we eat this bread and drink this cup, we proclaim your death, O Lord, until you come again" (see 1 Corinthians 11:26).

6. *Anamnesis.* Jesus told the apostles, his first priests, to celebrate the Eucharist "in remembrance of me" (Luke 22:19, 1 Corinthians 11:24–25). The Greek word for remembrance is *anamnesis*, and so the priest now recites a part of the eucharistic prayer that commemorates God's saving actions in history, especially the life, death, and Resurrection of Christ.

7. *Oblation (Offering).* Because the Eucharist is a sacrifice, it involves a gift, or offering, that is given to God: Jesus Christ, who through the Eucharist continually offers himself to the Father in heaven. We also offer our-

selves to God in union with Jesus. The priest asks God to accept and bless our offering of ourselves together with Christ, fulfilling Paul's exhortation in Romans 12:1 that we Christians are to "present [our] bodies as a living sacrifice, holy and acceptable to God, which is [our] spiritual worship."

8. *Intercessions.* The priest then asks the Father to bless the whole Christian family—living and dead—to give us his mercy, and to bring us to the fullness of salvation in heaven.

9. *Concluding Doxology.* The eucharistic prayer comes to a close when the priest gives the final doxology and the people or choir respond, "Amen."

A *doxology* is a prayer that praises God's glory (Greek, *doxa*, "glory" + *logion*, "a speech"). In the final doxology, the priest summarizes all that has come before by giving glory to God through Christ, saying, "Through him, and with him, and in him, O God, in the unity of the Holy Spirit, all glory and honor is yours, for ever and ever." The people respond by saying or singing, "Amen," and stand.

Amen is a Hebrew word used to signify agreement with a prayer and confidence that God will hear and respond to it. This *Amen* is the most important part of the people's role in the eucharistic prayer, since they give their assent to what the priest has just prayed on their behalf. Because of its importance, this *Amen*, which is often sung, is also called "*the Great Amen.*"

D. *Communion Rite.* The congregation now prepares for and receives Jesus Christ in Holy Communion.

1. The *Lord's Prayer* (the *Our Father*). The Communion Rite begins with the praying of the Lord's Prayer, or Our Father, the model of all Christian prayer (Matthew 6:9–

13). It asks for "our daily bread," the food that sustains our physical lives, and, in a spiritual sense, for Christ himself, the "Bread from Heaven" (John 6:32, 41) that sustains our spiritual lives (John 6:51). The Lord's Prayer also petitions for forgiveness for our sins. We must have this forgiveness if we are to receive Jesus in Communion (1 Corinthians 11:27–28).

After the conclusion of the Lord's Prayer, the priest briefly prays for God to deliver all of us from every evil. The people then say to God, "For the kingdom, the power, and the glory are yours, now and forever." These words were not originally part of the Lord's Prayer (they are not in the earliest Scripture manuscripts). There are, however, early Christian writings, such as the first-century document known as the *Didache*, showing that such words were used in the liturgy in the early Church.

2. The *Rite of Peace*. The priest then prays that Christ will "look not on our sins, but on the faith of your Church, and graciously grant her peace and unity in accordance with your will." In many parishes the priest or deacon invites the congregation to exchange a "sign of peace" (for example, a handshake) with those around them as a symbol of their peace and unity with each other in Christ. The apostles regularly exhorted their congregations to be at peace and of one mind (1 Corinthians 1:10, Philippians 1:27, 2:2), and Jesus himself warned us to be reconciled with our brethren prior to coming before God (Matthew 5:23–24), making the Rite of Peace a fitting preparation for Communion.

3. The *Fraction*. Reflecting Jesus' actions at the Last Supper, when he broke the bread (Luke 22:19), the priest then breaks (fractions) the consecrated host, symboliz-

ing the breaking of Christ's body on the cross. He drops a small part of the host into the chalice, symbolizing the Resurrection of Christ (reuniting body and blood as a living whole). Because all of the living Jesus is present both under the appearances of bread and wine, the priest's action does not actually separate and reunite Jesus' body and blood; it does so symbolically.

While the priest is doing this, a prayer called the *Agnus Dei* (Latin, "Lamb of God") is said or sung. This prayer asks Jesus Christ, the "Lamb of God, [who takes] away the sins of the world," to "have mercy on us" and "grant us peace."

4. *Communion.* The priest begins the communion rite with a quiet prayer to prepare himself to receive Communion. He then holds up the Eucharist to the faithful, proclaiming, "Behold the Lamb of God, behold him who takes away the sins of the world. Blessed are those called to the supper of the Lamb." Then, echoing the words of the Roman centurion in Matthew 8:8, all pray, "Lord, I am not worthy that you should enter under my roof, but only say the word and my soul shall be healed." In many parishes, people kneel during this exchange as a sign of their reverence for Christ.

The priest then receives Communion and, often with the assistance of other ministers, such as the deacon, he begins to distribute Communion to the faithful.

Each communicant is shown the host before receiving it, as the words "The Body of Christ" are intoned. The reply, "Amen," is a confession of faith in the Real Presence of Christ. When Communion is also being offered from the chalice, the words intoned are "The Blood of Christ." The reply of faith in the Real Presence is again "Amen."

(As has been noted, the entire Christ—his body, blood, soul, and divinity—is really present under the appearances of both bread and wine; however, the appearances of bread are a special sign of his Body, and the appearances of wine are a special sign of his Blood.)

In many parishes a hymn is sung during the distribution of Communion.

5. *Prayer after Communion*. After the faithful have received Communion they return to their places to pray and give thanks to God for the wonderful gift of receiving his Son in such a miraculous and intimate manner. Afterwards, the priest offers a concluding prayer to complete the private prayer of the people and to close the Communion Rite. This is referred to as the "Prayer After Communion".

IV. CONCLUDING RITES

Following the Liturgy of the Eucharist are the Concluding Rites. Being less important than what has come before, they tend to be brief.

A. *Announcements*. Many times, special announcements of parish news need to be made—for example, of upcoming parish events. These may be made at this time.

B. *Greeting*. After the announcements (if any), the priest greets the people with customary words, such as "The Lord be with you," to which everyone responds, "And with your spirit."

C. *Blessing*. The priest then gives a blessing to the people (just as priests did in the Bible; Numbers 6:22–27). This may be done in a simple or a solemn manner. When it is done solemnly, the priest or deacon begins by instructing the people, "Bow your heads and pray for

God's blessing," after which a more elaborate blessing is said over them. Whether the blessing is done simply or solemnly, however, the priest always concludes by making the sign of the cross over the people, saying, "May almighty God bless you, the Father, the Son, and the Holy Spirit." All respond, "Amen."

D. *Dismissal.* After the blessing, the people are dismissed to go out and do good in their lives, based on the grace and empowerment they have received at Mass. The priest or deacon dismisses them by using a formula such as "Go forth, the Mass is ended," to which all respond, "Thanks be to God."

It is actually this dismissal that gives the *Mass* its name. The Latin word *missio* ("sending forth") became part of the priest's or deacon's statement "Go, the Mass is ended" (Latin, *Ite, missa est.* Literally, "Go, it has been sent"). This sending forth came to be used as a name for the whole worship service.

E. *Veneration of the Altar.* Before departing, the priest shows his reverence to God by honoring the place where Christ comes to us in the Eucharist. He does so by kissing the altar and making a profound bow with the other ministers. Often while this is happening, the choir or congregation sings a concluding hymn.

7. LEARNING MORE

This booklet is meant to help you learn the basics of the Mass. But the topic is rich and deep and important, more profound than any booklet could help you fully appreciate. You may wish to go deeper into the subject and learn more. I particularly recommend the following valuable resources:

Catechism of the Catholic Church
(New York: Doubleday, 1995)
A catechism is a book that teaches the basics of the faith. This catechism is the most important and influential of all. It is the Church's most official, worldwide catechism, featuring an excellent section on the Mass and the liturgy as well as the other aspects of the faith. For some, this catechism may be a bit difficult at first, so it is good to use other catechisms too. But this one cannot be too highly recommended. References in this booklet to numbered paragraphs in the Catechism of the Catholic Church are preceded by the abbreviation CCC.

Akin, Jimmy. Mass Revision: How the Liturgy Is Changing and What It Means for You (San Diego: Catholic Answers, 2011)
Because the Mass is so important, the Church has rules about how it is to be performed. I wrote this book to answer the questions of people who want to know what those rules are.

Groeschel, Benedict, C.F.R., and James Monti.
In the Presence of Our Lord
(Huntington, Indiana: Our Sunday Visitor, 1997)
Because Jesus is really present in the Eucharist, Christians have long wanted to honor him in the Eucharist, both during and outside of Mass. In this book, the authors explain the history and meaning of devotion to Jesus in the Eucharist and offer practical aids for helping us honor Jesus more in the Eucharist.

Howard, Thomas. *If Your Mind Wanders at Mass*
(San Francisco: Ignatius, 2001)
Because we are fallen human beings, our minds wander. We don't always have the concentration we want, and

we don't always appreciate what we should. Thomas Howard wrote this excellent, short book to help people who find themselves distracted when they want to be worshiping God.

APPENDIX
GUIDELINES FOR THE RECEPTION OF COMMUNION

On November 14, 1996, the National Conference of Catholic Bishops approved the following guidelines on the reception of Communion. These guidelines replace the guidelines approved by the Administrative Committee of the NCCB in November 1986. The guidelines, which are to be included in missalettes and other participation aids published in the United States, seek to remind all those who may attend Catholic liturgies of the present discipline of the Church with regard to the sharing of eucharistic Communion.

FOR CATHOLICS
As Catholics, we fully participate in the celebration of the Eucharist when we receive Holy Communion. We are encouraged to receive Communion devoutly and frequently. In order to be properly disposed to receive Communion, participants should not be conscious of grave sin and normally should have fasted for one hour. A person who is conscious of grave sin is not to receive the Body and Blood of the Lord without prior sacramental confession except for a grave reason where there is no opportunity for confession. In this case, the person is to be mindful of the obligation to make an act of perfect contrition, including the intention of confessing as soon as possible (canon 916). A frequent reception of the sacrament of penance is encouraged for all.

FOR OUR FELLOW CHRISTIANS
We welcome our fellow Christians to this celebration of the Eucharist as our brothers and sisters. We pray that

our common baptism and the action of the Holy Spirit in this Eucharist will draw us closer to one another and begin to dispel the sad divisions which separate us. We pray that these will lessen and finally disappear, in keeping with Christ's prayer for us "that they may all be one" (Jn 17:21).

Because Catholics believe that the celebration of the Eucharist is a sign of the reality of the oneness of faith, life, and worship, members of those churches with whom we are not yet fully united are ordinarily not admitted to Holy Communion. Eucharistic sharing in exceptional circumstances by other Christians requires permission according to the directives of the diocesan bishop and the provisions of canon law (canon 844 § 4). Members of the Orthodox Churches, the Assyrian Church of the East, and the Polish National Catholic Church are urged to respect the discipline of their own Churches. According to Roman Catholic discipline, the Code of Canon Law does not object to the reception of Communion by Christians of these Churches (canon 844 § 3).

FOR THOSE NOT RECEIVING HOLY COMMUNION
All who are not receiving Holy Communion are encouraged to express in their hearts a prayerful desire for unity with the Lord Jesus and with one another.

FOR NON-CHRISTIANS
We also welcome to this celebration those who do not share our faith in Jesus Christ. While we cannot admit them to Holy Communion, we ask them to offer their prayers for the peace and the unity of the human family.

OUTLINE OF THE MASS

I. Introductory Rites
   A. Entrance
   B. Veneration of the Altar
   C. Greeting
   D. Penitential Act
   E. *Kyrie*
   F. Blessing and Sprinkling
   G. *Gloria*
   H. Collect

II. Liturgy of the Word
   A. Scripture Readings
   B. Homily
   C. Profession of Faith
   D. Prayer of the Faithful

III. Liturgy of the Eucharist
   A. Preparation of the Gifts
   B. Prayer over the Offerings
   C. Eucharistic Prayer
      1. Thanksgiving (Preface)
      2. Acclamation (*Sanctus*)
      3. *Epiclesis*
      4. Institution Narrative and Consecration
      5. Memorial Acclamation
      6. *Anamnesis*
      7. Offering
      8. Intercessions
      9. Final Doxology
   D. Communion Rite
      1. Lord's Prayer
      2. Rite of Peace
      3. Fraction
      4. Communion
      5. Prayer after Communion

IV. Concluding Rites
   A. Announcements
   B. Greeting
   C. Blessing
   D. Dismissal
   E. Veneration of the Altar

INDEX

What Is Catholic Answers?

Catholic Answers is a media ministry that serves Christ by explaining and defending the Catholic faith:

- We help Catholics grow in their faith
- We bring former Catholics home
- We lead non-Catholics into the fullness of the truth

There are many ways we help people:

 Catholic Answers Live is America's most popular Catholic radio program

 Catholic Answers Press publishes faith-building books, booklets, magazines, and audio resources

 Catholic Answers Studios creates television programs, DVDs, and online videos

 Our website, Catholic.com hosts hundreds of thousands of online resources, free to use

 Catholic Answers Events conducts seminars, conferences, and pilgrimages

Catholic Answers is an independent, nonprofit organization supported by your donations.

Visit us online and learn how we can help you.

Your journey starts at:
catholic.com